Lerner SPORTS

ALL-STAR SMACKDOWN

TRINITY RODMAN VS. CARLI LLOYD

WHO WOULD WIN?

KELLEY BARTH

Lerner Publications ◆ Minneapolis

The stats and information in this book are accurate through April 2025.

Lerner Publications Company
An imprint of Lerner Publishing Group, Inc.
241 First Avenue North
Minneapolis, MN 55401 USA

For reading levels and more information, look up this title at www.lernerbooks.com.

Main body text set in Aptifer Sans LT Pro.
Typeface provided by Linotype AG.

Library of Congress Cataloging-in-Publication Data

Names: Barth, Kelley author
Title: Trinity Rodman vs. Carli Lloyd : who would win? / by Kelley Barth.
Other titles: Trinity Rodman versus Carli Lloyd
Description: Minneapolis : Lerner Publications, [2026] | Series: Lerner Sports. All-star smackdown | Includes bibliographical references and index. | Audience: Ages 7–11 | Audience: Grades 2–3 | Summary: "Trinity Rodman and Carli Lloyd are all-time great soccer players. But which on is the best? Readers discover exciting moments, key stats, impressive wins, and decide for themselves who comes out on top"—Provided by publisher.
Identifiers: LCCN 2025011520 (print) | LCCN 2025011521 (ebook) | ISBN 9798765689462 lib. bdg. | ISBN 9798348028404 pbk | ISBN 9798765694381 epub
Subjects: LCSH: Women soccer players—Rating of—United States—Juvenile literature | Soccer midfielders—United States—Statistics—Juvenile literature | Rodman, Trinity, 2002– | Lloyd, Carli, 1982– | Sports rivalries—United States—History—Juvenile literature | LCGFT: Statistics
Classification: LCC GV942.7.A1 B38 2026 (print) | LCC GV942.7.A1 (ebook) | DDC 796.334092/52—dc23/eng/20250605

LC record available at https://lccn.loc.gov/2025011520
LC ebook record available at https://lccn.loc.gov/2025011521

Manufactured in the United States of America
1 – CG – 12/15/25

TABLE OF CONTENTS

Carli Lloyd

INTRODUCTION

SOCCER SUPERSTARS

It was the final match of the 2015 FIFA Women's World Cup. Millions of fans tuned in to watch the US Women's National Team (USWNT) play Japan. The pressure was on. But midfielder Carli Lloyd was used to playing under pressure.

FAST FACTS

- Carli Lloyd is a two-time FIFA Player of the Year.
- Throughout her career, Lloyd played 316 games with the USWNT.
- Trinity Rodman won the National Women's Soccer League (NWSL) Rookie of the Year award in 2021.
- Rodman scored three total goals at the 2024 Olympics to help the US bring home a gold medal.

Less than three minutes into the game, Lloyd scored. It was the fastest goal ever scored in a Women's World Cup Final. Two minutes later, she scored again, extending the US's lead 2–0.

Eleven minutes later, Lloyd sent another powerful kick sailing into the air. It soared over the Japanese goaltender's head to score Lloyd's third goal of the game. She was the first woman to score a hat trick in a World Cup Final. It was also the fastest any player had ever done so.

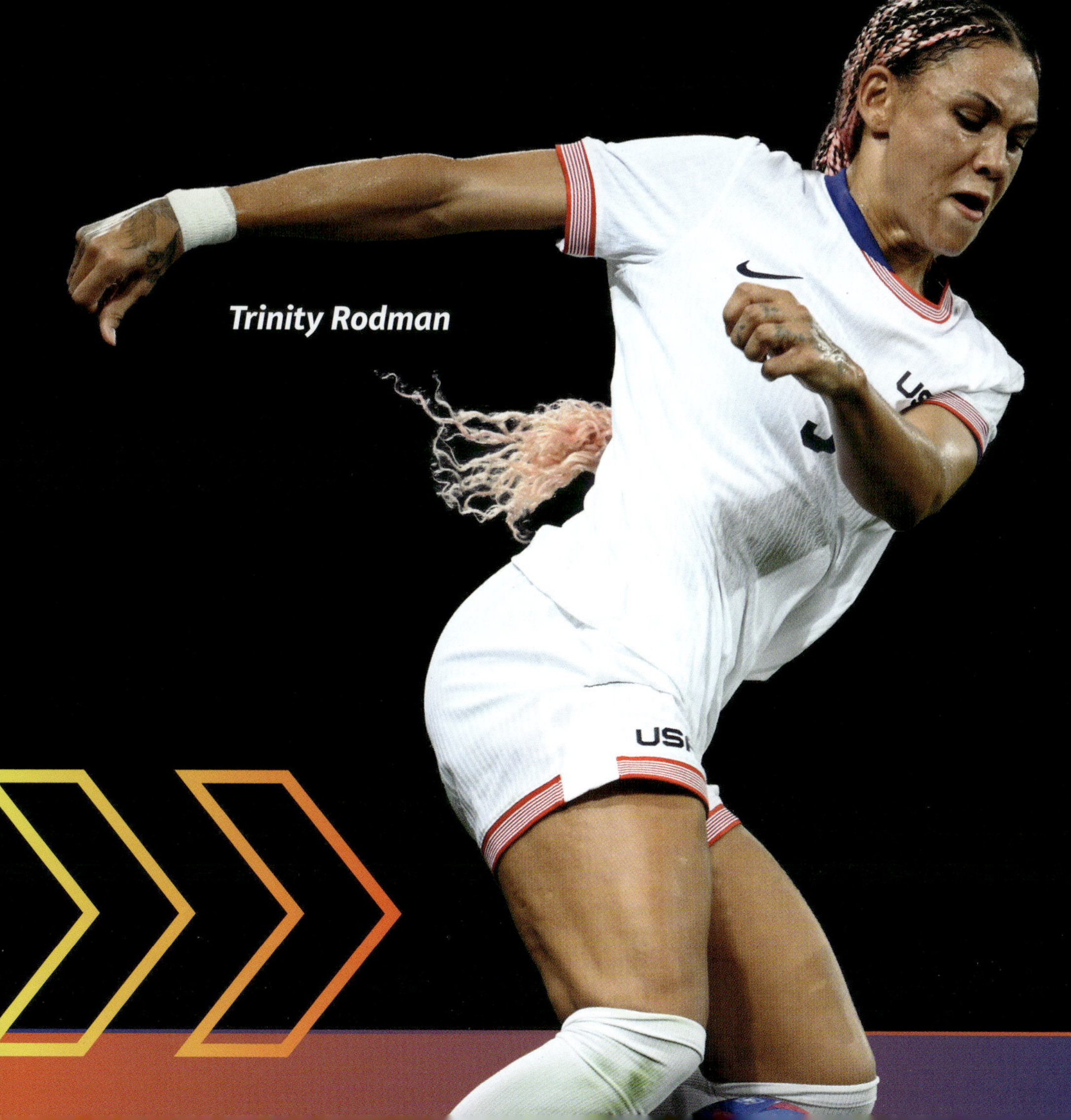

Trinity Rodman

The US won 5–2. It was their first World Cup win in 16 years. Lloyd scored a total of six goals in the tournament.

Nine years later, it was Trinity Rodman's time to shine at the 2024 Olympics. She had joined the USWNT just two years earlier and was one of the youngest members of the team. In the 17th minute of the US's first match against Zambia, Rodman skillfully dribbled her way around two opponents and scored the USWNT's first goal of the tournament. She went on to score two more goals for the US during her first Olympic games.

Lloyd and Rodman are both great forwards who can be counted on to score big goals. But who is the best? Let the smackdown begin!

Lloyd earned multiple World Cup trophies during her career.

Rodman celebrates scoring her first Olympic goal during a match against Zambia in 2024.

CHAPTER 1

Lloyd started playing for the USWNT in 2005.

JOURNEY TO SUCCESS

Carli Lloyd was born on July 16, 1982, in New Jersey. She started playing soccer at age five. Her parents encouraged her to try ballet instead.

But Lloyd insisted that soccer was the sport for her. When she was 16, she watched the USWNT play in the opening match of the 1999 World Cup. Lloyd was inspired by the excitement of the crowd. She realized that maybe she could become a professional soccer player someday.

In 2001, Lloyd enrolled at Rutgers University. She started gaining attention for her athletic skills. She was selected for the All-Big East First Team all four years of college. This is a team of the very best players in her conference. It was the first time in history that someone from Rutgers made the First Team four years in a row.

Lloyd was captain of the UNWNT from 2016 until 2020.

By the time she graduated, Lloyd had scored a school record 50 goals for the team. She had proven her skills and was ready for the next step in her career.

Trinity Rodman was born on May 20, 2002, in California. She also found her talent for soccer at a young age. Rodman started playing at age four and quickly fell in love with the sport. Her mom encouraged her to follow her passion. Rodman played in a youth league growing up. She and her team went five years without a single loss.

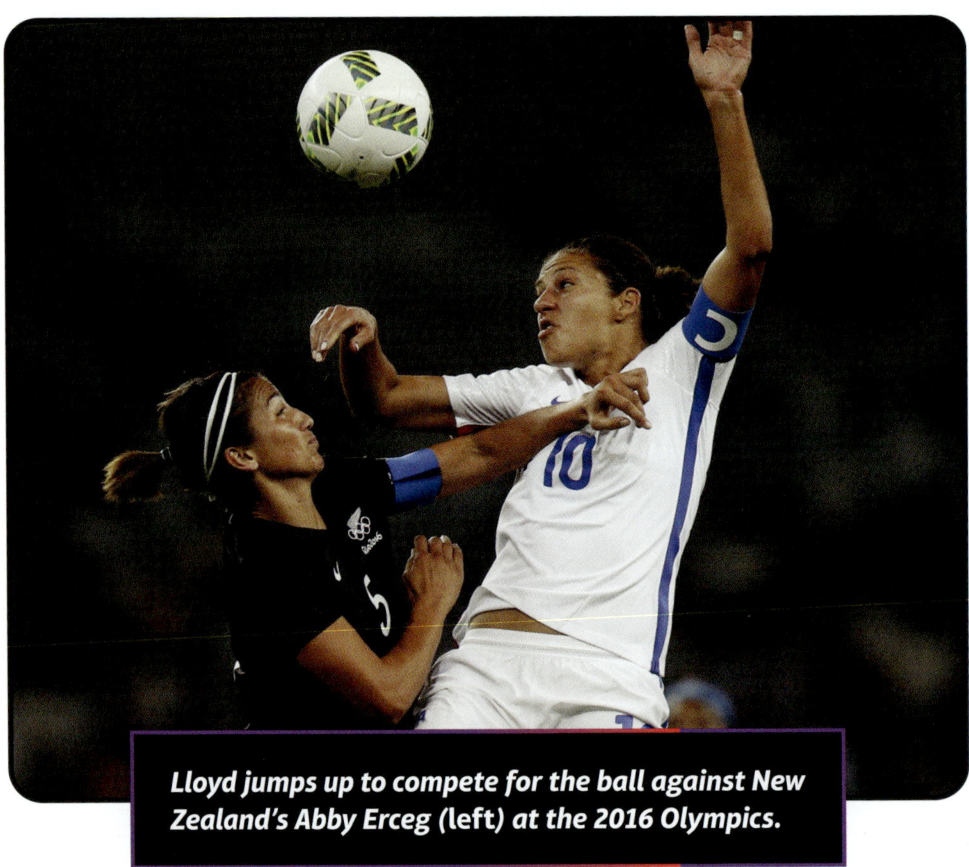

Lloyd jumps up to compete for the ball against New Zealand's Abby Erceg (left) at the 2016 Olympics.

Rodman during a 2017 match for the US's under-16 team.

CONSIDER THIS

Both Lloyd and Rodman played on US national youth teams when they were younger. Lloyd was part of the under-21 team for four years before joining the USWNT. Rodman spent time on the under-16, under-17, and under-20 teams before being called up.

Rodman goes in for a kick against Germany's Nina Schumacher (left) in 2017.

College coaches noticed Rodman's skills. She decided to play for Washington State University, where her older brother played basketball. Unfortunately, her freshman season didn't work out as planned. The 2020 fall soccer season was canceled because of the COVID-19 pandemic.

Rodman was disappointed. But she wasn't about to give up. Instead, she signed up for the 2021 NWSL draft. If she couldn't play in college, she would go pro instead.

Rodman celebrates a goal after scoring for the Washington Spirit in 2021.

CHAPTER 2

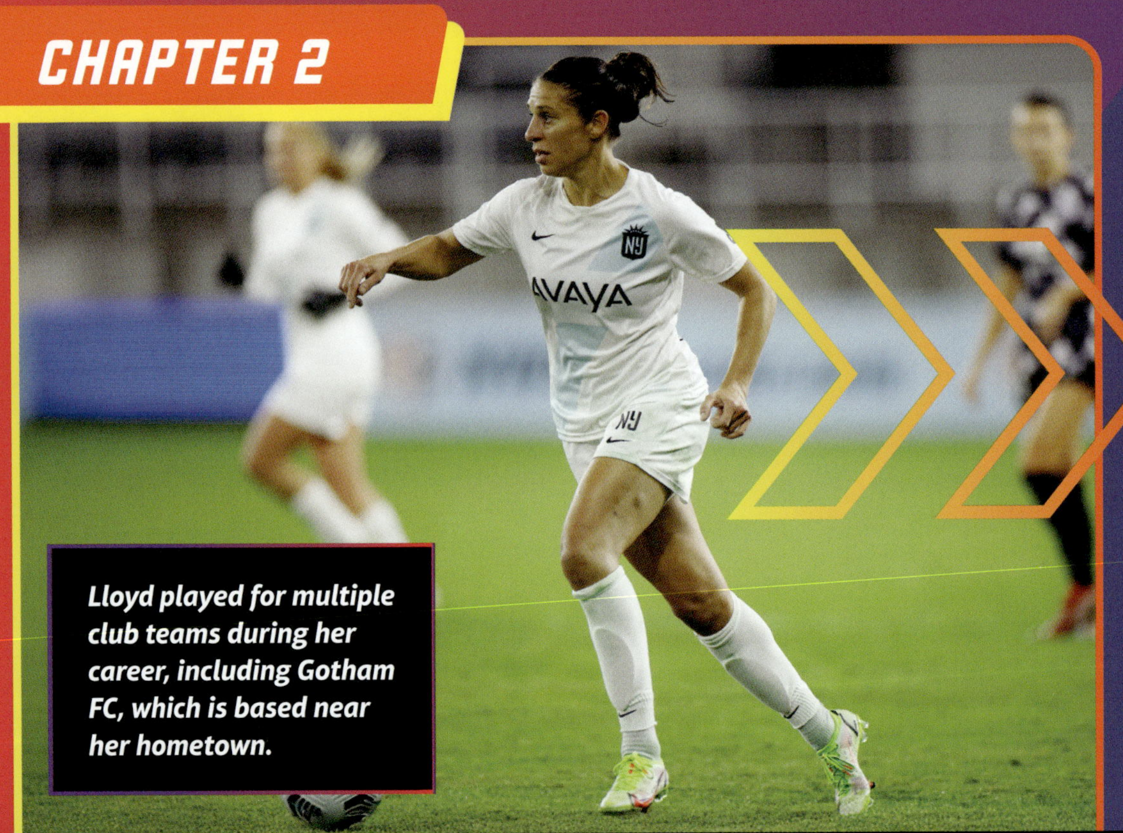

Lloyd played for multiple club teams during her career, including Gotham FC, which is based near her hometown.

GREAT MOMENTS

Carli Lloyd joined the USWNT in 2005. She got off to a strong start. At the 2007 Algarve Cup, Lloyd scored four goals, including two in one match. She was the tournament's top scorer and won the Most Valuable Player award.

A year later at her first Olympics, Lloyd continued to impress. She had already scored the game-winning goal against Japan earlier in the tournament. But now the US faced Brazil in the final, and a gold medal was on the line.

CONSIDER THIS

For a long time, female soccer players weren't paid as much as male players. Carli Lloyd and her teammates decided that wasn't fair. They fought for fair pay for all players. In the end, they reached an agreement with US Soccer that male and female players would be paid equally.

Lloyd (back right) celebrates her 2008 Olympic gold medal win with her teammates.

Lloyd battles it out against Brazil's Ester at the 2008 Olympics.

The game went into overtime and the teams were still tied 0–0. But Lloyd finally found her opening. She scored the game's only goal and won her first Olympic gold medal. Four years later, Lloyd repeated her Olympic success. In the final match against Japan, she scored two goals for the US. Once again, she led the team to victory and earned her second gold medal.

In 2021, the NWSL's Washington Spirit drafted Trinity Rodman. She was the second player selected in the draft. At the time, Rodman was the youngest player drafted in the history of the NWSL. She was only 18 years old. But her age didn't hold her back.

Rodman won the US Soccer Young Female Player of the Year award in 2021.

Five minutes into her first game for the Spirit, Rodman scored a goal. Rodman scored the second-most goals on the team that season. She scored seven goals and had seven assists. Rodman also helped lead the Spirit to their first NWSL championship. They beat the Chicago Red Stars 2–1 in the final.

Rodman winds up for a kick during a Washington Spirit game in 2021.

Rodman keeps her eye on the ball during a 2022 match for the Washington Spirit.

Rodman followed up her rookie year with more great moments. Throughout 2022 and 2023, Rodman played in 37 matches for the Spirit and 28 matches for the USWNT. She scored two goals for the USWNT in a match against Wales before the 2023 World Cup.

CHAPTER 3

Rodman controls the ball during a 2024 match for the USWNT.

FANTASTIC FORWARDS

Lloyd and Rodman have both impressed on the field. Carli Lloyd played 316 games with USWNT. That is the second-most of all time. She also holds the record for the third-most USWNT goals of all time with 134. She is tied for the fifth-most assists with 64. Trinity Rodman hasn't been with the team as long. But with 46 USWNT games, 10 goals, and nine assists, she has made an impressive start.

Both players have proven themselves on the international

stage. Even after her historic hat trick at the 2015 World Cup, Lloyd continued making a name for herself. In 2019, Lloyd and the USWNT won another World Cup.

In 2021, Lloyd made her fourth Olympic appearance. After losing early in the tournament at the 2016 Olympics, the USWNT was determined to do better. Lloyd scored two goals in the bronze medal match against Australia. Lloyd announced in 2021 that she was retiring from soccer.

Over her four Olympic appearances, Lloyd earned three medals, including two gold, and scored 10 goals. No other US player has scored that many goals at the Olympics.

Lloyd prepares for a kick during the bronze medal match against Australia in the 2021 Olympics.

CONSIDER THIS

Women's soccer was added to the Olympics in 1996. Since that time, the US has won five gold medals.

Rodman played in her first Olympics in 2024 and helped the US bring home gold. So far, she has scored three Olympic goals and made one assist. Lloyd has also won two World Cups. While Rodman was part of the USWNT at the 2023 World Cup, the US failed to place after losing to Sweden in a penalty kick shootout.

Throughout her career, Lloyd found great success in the USWNT, while Rodman has more accomplishments in club soccer. Lloyd was named FIFA's top female player of the year

Lloyd accepts her 2015 FIFA Player of the Year award alongside Lionel Messi (right).

in both 2015 and 2016. Rodman won the NWSL Rookie of the Year award in 2021. Rodman also made the Best 11 list in both 2021 and 2024. That is a list of the 11 best players in the league for the season.

In 2024, Rodman broke the Washington Spirit record for the most career assists. She was also tied for the most goals on the team that year with eight. But Rodman didn't just play for the Spirit that year. She joined the USWNT at her first Olympic Games in France. The US and Japan were tied 0–0 in the quarterfinals when Rodman shot the ball into the upper corner of the net during overtime. She called it the best moment of her career—so far. Rodman's goal was the game winner, and the USWNT went on to beat Brazil for the gold medal.

Rodman shows off her gold medal after the 2024 Olympics.

CHAPTER 4

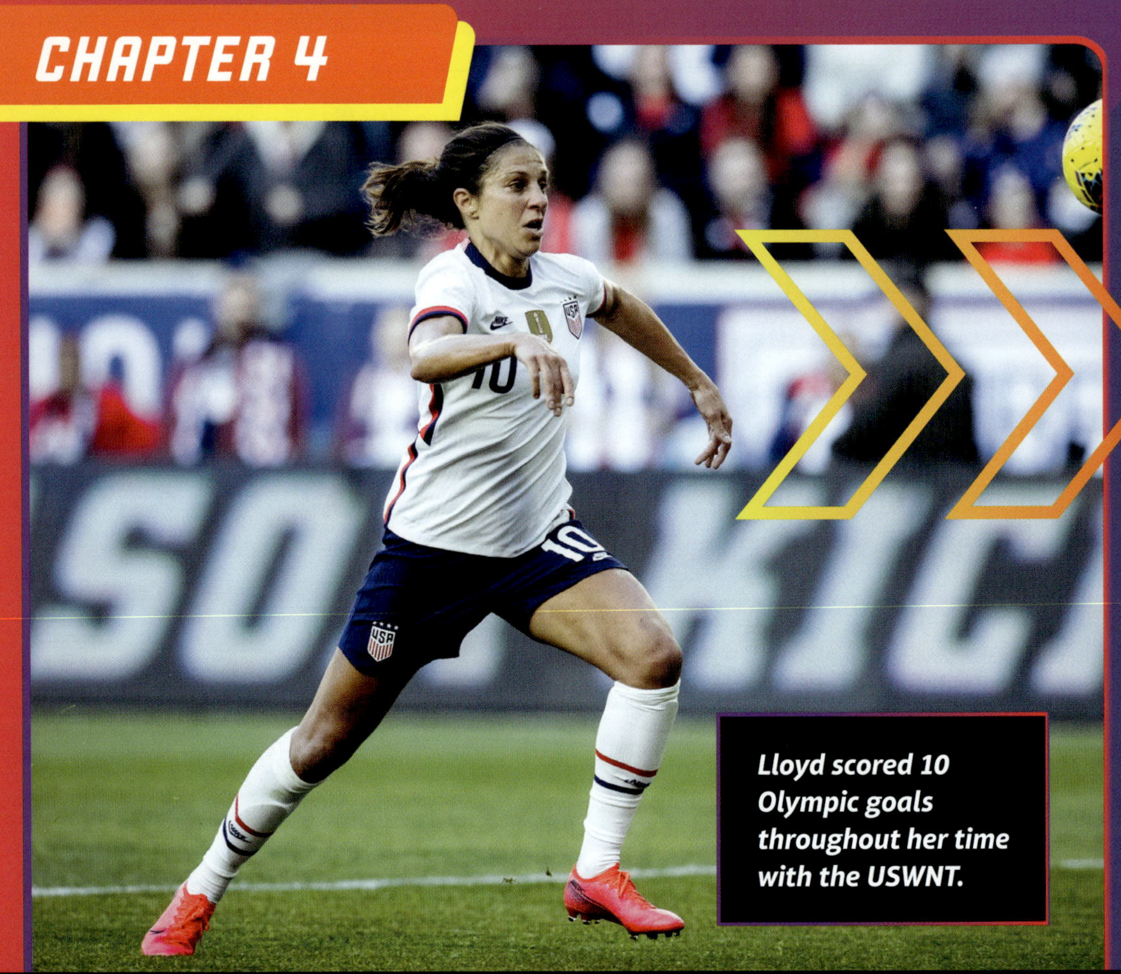

Lloyd scored 10 Olympic goals throughout her time with the USWNT.

AND THE WINNER IS

So who wins this smackdown? It is a tight matchup. Both players have proven their talent. Carli Lloyd was known for being able to play multiple positions. She holds the record for the second-most USWNT appearances of all time. She helped lead her team to two Olympic gold medals and one bronze. She also has won two World Cups. In 2025, she became part of the National Soccer Hall of Fame.

Trinity Rodman is newer to the game. She hasn't yet put in the number of appearances that Lloyd did. But Rodman has already made her mark. She is known for her smart and skillful ball handling. She even has a signature move that was named after her: the Trin Spin. Rodman has also already won an Olympic gold medal and an NWSL championship in the first few years of her career.

Rodman battles Sweden's Magdalena Eriksson (right) for control of the ball during the 2023 World Cup.

Rodman is a talented player who will likely go on to have a long, successful career. But we're giving this smackdown to Carli Lloyd, who has proven herself to be one of the all-time greats. But ask again in 10 years, because you never know what could happen in an all-star smackdown.

Do you agree with this choice? Think about each player's accomplishments. Consider their stats. Decide for yourself who the winner should be!

Rodman was a finalist for the US Soccer Female Player of the Year award in 2024.

Lloyd waves goodbye to the crowd after a 2021 match for the USWNT.

SMACKDOWN BREAKDOWN

CARLI LLOYD

Height: 5 feet 8 (1.7 m)
Olympic medals: 3 (2 gold; 1 bronze)
FIFA World Cups: 2
Number of appearances for
US national team: 316

TRINITY RODMAN

Height: 5 feet 7 (1.7 m)
Olympic medals: 1 (gold)
FIFA World Cups: 0
Number of appearances for US national team: 46 and counting

GLOSSARY

appearance: having played in a game

assist: a pass from a teammate that leads directly to a goal

conference: a group of teams that play one another

draft: when teams take turns choosing new players

hat trick: three goals scored in a game by one person

midfielder: a player who plays both offense and defense in the central area of the field between the forwards and defenders

opponent: a player on the other team

overtime: extra time added to a game when the score is tied at the end of the normal playing time

rookie: a player in their first year

LEARN MORE

About Carli Lloyd
https://carlilloyd.com/pages/about-carli

Schwartz, Heather E. *US Women's National Soccer Team: Winning On and Off the Field*. Lerner Publications, 2024.

Shaw, Gina. *What Is the Women's World Cup?* Penguin Workshop, 2023.

Smith, Charles R. *Soccer Queens*. Candlewick Press, 2023.

Trinity Rodman Facts for Kids
https://kids.kiddle.co/Trinity_Rodman

United States Women's National Soccer Team Facts for Kids
https://kids.kiddle.co/United_States_women%27s_national_soccer_team

INDEX

PHOTO ACKNOWLEDGMENTS

Image credits: Pedro Vilela/Getty Images, p. 4; Stuart Franklin - FIFA/FIFA/Getty Images, p. 5; Mike Hewitt - FIFA/FIFA/Getty Images, p. 6; Stuart Franklin - FIFA/FIFA/Getty Images, p. 7; Scott Bales/Icon SMI 918/Newscom, p. 8; Omar Vega/Getty Images, p. 9; Joern Pollex - FIFA/FIFA/Getty Images, p. 10; Oliver Hardt/Bongarts/Getty Images, p. 11; Oliver Hardt/Bongarts/Getty Images, p. 12; Brad Smith/ISI Photos/Getty Images, p. 13; Joe Robbins/ISI Photos/Getty Images, p. 14; Ryan Pierse/Getty Images, p. 15; Cameron Spencer/Getty Images, p. 16; Justin Satterfield/Getty Images, p. 17; Tony Quinn/ISI Photos/USSF/Getty Images, p. 18; Scott Taetsch/Getty Images, p. 19; Brad Smith/ISI Photos/USSF/Getty Images, p. 20; Brad Smith/ISI Photos/Getty Images, p. 21; FABRICE CONFFRINI/AFP/Getty Images, p. 22; Kristy Sparrow/Getty Images, p. 23; Ira L. Black/Corbis/Getty Images, p. 24; Jose Breton/Pics Action/NurPhoto/Getty Images, p. 25; Brad Smith/ISI Photos/USSF/Getty Images, p. 26; Emilee Chinn/Getty Images, p. 27; Robson Alma/Icon Sportswire/Getty Images, p. 28; Alex Livesey/Getty Images, p. 29.

Cover: Randy Litzinger/Icon Sportswire/Newscom; Trask Smith/Cal Sport Media/Newscom